Tundra

by Susan H. Gray

Content Adviser: Terrence E. Young Jr., M.Ed., M.L.S.,
Jefferson Parish (La.) Public Schools

Reading Adviser: Dr. Linda D. Labbo,
Department of Reading Education, College of Education,
The University of Georgia

COMPASS POINT BOOKS

Minneapolis, Minnesota

FIRST REPORTS

C.1
Great Plains
Polar themes

Compass Point Books
3722 West 50th Street, #115
Minneapolis, MN 55410

Visit Compass Point Books on the Internet at *www.compasspointbooks.com* or e-mail your request to *custserv@compasspointbooks.com*

Photographs ©: Visuals Unlimited/Patric Endres, cover; Root Resources/Kenneth W. Fink, 4; Unicorn Stock Photos/Dick Keen, 5; Visuals Unlimited/Leonard Lee Rue III, 6; Root Resources/Kitty Kohout, 7; Index Stock Imagery, 8, 9; International Stock/Eric Sanford, 10; Visuals Unlimited/Jeannette Thomas, 11; Unicorn Stock Photos/Andre Jenny, 12; Visuals Unlimited/Tim Hauf Photography, 13; Mary Clay/Colephoto, 15; Visuals Unlimited/Patrick J. Endres, 16; Mark Newman/Tom Stack and Associates, 17; Visuals Unlimited/Steve McCutcheon, 18, 19 top and bottom; Visuals Unlimited/John Sohlden, 20; Index Stock Imagery/Bob Lienemann, 22; Bob and Ira Spring, 23; Root Resources/Kohout Productions, 24; Rod Planck/Tom Stack and Associates, 25; John Shaw/Tom Stack and Associates, 26 top and bottom; Robert McCaw, 27; Visuals Unlimited/Rich Poley, 28; Robert McCaw, 29; Visuals Unlimited/Gary Meszaros, 30; Visuals Unlimited/Joe McDonald, 31; Visuals Unlimited/Lindholm, 32 top; Visuals Unlimited/Rick Baetsen, 32 bottom; Visuals Unlimited/William J. Weber, 33; Erwin and Peggy Bauer/Tom Stack and Associates, 34; Photo Network/Mark Newman, 35; Jonathan Blair/Corbis, 36; Reuters NewMedia, Inc./Corbis, 37; Nancy Carter/North Wind Picture Archives, 38; Reuters NewMedia, Inc./Corbis, 39; Dean Conger/Corbis, 40; Index Stock Imagery, 42.

Editors: E. Russell Primm and Emily J. Dolbear
Photo Researcher: Svetlana Zhurkina
Photo Selector: Dawn Friedman
Design: Bradfordesign, Inc.

Library of Congress Cataloging-in-Publication Data
Gray, Susan Heinrichs.
    Tundra / by Susan H. Gray.
       p. cm. — (First reports)
    Includes bibliographical references and index.
    Summary: Briefly describes the climate, land formations, plant life, and animals of the frozen arctic land called tundra.
    ISBN 0-7565-0024-9 (hardcover : lib. bdg.)
      1. Tundra ecology—Juvenile literature. 2. Tundras—Juvenile literature. [1. Tundra ecology. 2. Ecology. 3. Tundras.] I. Title. II. Series.
    QH541.5.T8 G73 2000
    577.5'86—dc21

00-008535

Table of Contents

What Is Tundra?

Questions about tundra often sound like riddles. For example: What gets little rainfall but its ground is soaked with water? Where does a moss that's not actually a moss grow? Where do hares called snow-shoe rabbits hop? What makes up much of Greenland, a country that is barely green at all? What is found around the Arctic Ocean, but doesn't include

△ *The Arctic tundra of northern Canada*

▲ *Reindeer moss is actually a lichen, not a moss.*

Arctic lands? The answer to all these questions is: tundra.

Some things about tundra are as clear as day though. The tundra has very cold temperatures and little rain or snow falls there. On the tundra, rainfall

takes a long time to **evaporate**, or rise into the air as a gas. It is warm enough for plants and many animals to live there too.

What Kind of Tundra?

▲ *Arctic tundra and mountains in Alaska*

There are two kinds of tundra: arctic tundra and alpine tundra. Arctic tundra is found in Alaska, Greenland, and the northern parts of Canada, Russia, and Europe. Alpine tundra is found at the tops of high mountains all over the world.

△ *The tundra of Lapland, Finland*

During the summer, the sun shines on the arctic tundra up to twenty-four hours each day. People call that part of the world the Land of the Midnight Sun. In winter, the sun is hardly seen at all.

The eastern, southern, and western edges of Greenland are part of the arctic tundra. Farther inland

and to the north the land is covered with solid ice. When early explorers noticed plants growing near the coast, they called it Greenland. If they had explored farther, they might have named it something else, such as Coldland or Frozenland!

▲ *The midnight sun in Iceland*

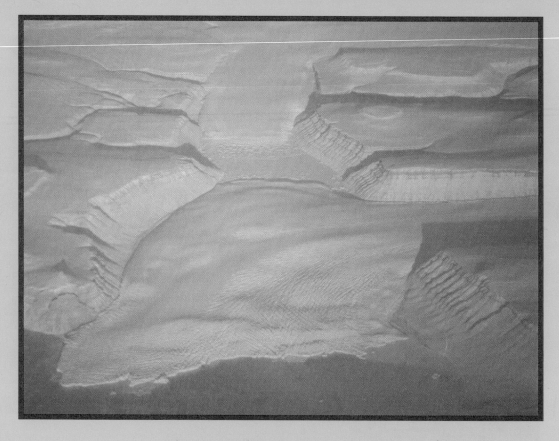

△ *Greenland's ice cap*

There is no antarctic tundra. It is too cold there for even tundra plants and animals. Antarctica is the only large landmass in the cold part of the southern half of the world.

Alpine tundra is found in the upper parts of mountains everywhere. In North America, alpine tundra can

▲ *No tundra grows in Antarctica.*

△ Alpine tundra in the Rocky Mountains, Colorado

be found in the Rocky Mountains, Appalachian Mountains, and Adirondack Mountains. Some alpine tundra is found in warm or tropical areas. Mountains in Central America, South America, Africa, and Hawaii have tundra areas. Unlike arctic tundra, alpine tundra gets about twelve hours of daylight all year round.

Trees cannot grow in the harsh cold and

▲ Alpine tundra in Peru

wind of alpine tundra or arctic tundra. But some tundra is near warmer areas with forests. South of the arctic tundra, the region slowly blends into forestland. Just below a mountain's alpine tundra where it is less windy and cold, trees are able to grow again.

The Frozen Ground

▲ *Tundra ponds still rimmed with ice, in Colorado*

As temperatures go up and down, the tundra's surface soil freezes and thaws. Below this, the soil is always frozen. This is called **permafrost**. There are a few patches of permafrost in alpine tundra. Very high places on the alpine tundra have a few patches of permafrost.

△ *Tundra bogs in Denali National Park, Alaska*

In arctic tundra, however, permafrost covers thousands of square miles and goes deep into the earth. In Barrow, Alaska, permafrost goes down more than 1,300 feet (397 meters) deep. Farther north, this frozen ground goes down more than 2,000 feet (610 meters).

When the weather warms up, the frozen soil above the permafrost melts. But the permafrost stays

▲ *Tundra thawing in Siberia, northern Russia*

frozen. The water from the thawing soil cannot soak into the ground, because permafrost blocks it.

Some plants may begin to grow in the area. The plants and the waterlogged soil make the ground marshy. This kind of land is called a **bog**.

Soil that freezes and thaws creates some strange landforms. In the summer, the temperature rises and

△ *A large pingo in northern Canada*

the ground melts. On a hillside, the mud slides down-hill. It flows unevenly and very slowly. Cold temperatures return quickly and then the mud freezes. It freezes into various landforms, such as **pingos** and **polygons**. Pingos are low hills caused by permafrost. Polygons are cracks in the land caused by the melting and freezing mud.

▼ Ice wedges caused these polygons.　　▲ An Alaskan pingo in front of the Brooks mountain range

The Tree Line

△ *High winds and cold temperatures slow the growth of trees at the tree line.*

The area between the tundra and forestland is called the **tree line**. On one side of this area stands a forest of tall evergreen trees. On the other side is the tundra with no trees at all. In between are short trees. They are short and twisted because of the cold, windy, dry weather.

In the Appalachian and Adirondack Mountains, the trees are so low and bent over that they look as if they are growing along the ground. They form a mat almost 3 feet (91 centimeters) deep and thick enough to walk on.

Plants on the Tundra

△ *Short plants grow in the alpine tundra of the San Juan Mountains, Colorado*

Because winters on the tundra are so long and cold, tundra plants have only a short time to grow. Many plants on the alpine tundra grow in a thick cushion close to the ground. This cushion traps the sun's heat. Inside the cushion, the temperatures may be more than 65° Fahrenheit (18° Celsius) warmer than out-side. Insects like these warm places.

For several months, the plants of the arctic tundra get sunlight all the time. They spring up quickly and send shallow roots into the soil. But the roots cannot grow deeply because they hit the solid permafrost.

▲ Shrub willow grows only one to two inches high in the tundra along the Arctic Ocean.

Most tundra plants are short sedges, heaths, grasses, mosses, and lichens. Sedges are flowering plants that look like grass. Heaths are woody shrubs. Mosses are small plants that need wet soil to grow.

A lichen is actually two plants living together. In a lichen, a plant called an alga makes food for another plant called a fungus.

△ Heaths

▲ *Lichen-covered rock*

Lichens have no roots. They grow on rocks or trees. They can look flaky, lacy, or hairy. They grow very slowly and live for a long time. A lichen in Greenland is more than 4,500 years old! The plant called reindeer moss is actually a common lichen in the arctic tundra.

▽ *Bearberry and lichens*   △ *Lichens and mosses growing on boulders*

Animals Big and Small

▲ *A white-veined Arctic butterfly*

Few insects can live on the tundra. But when the land is wet and muddy, swarms of mosquitoes come out. Mosquitoes lay their eggs in water, and arctic bogs are the perfect places. Butterflies and grasshoppers live in the alpine tundra. Because it is so windy, but-terflies stay very near the ground.

In summer, the arctic tundra is dotted with lakes and bogs. These attract many birds. Most are water-birds such as sandpipers and plovers. Their long,

△ A plover

▲ *Whimbrels are birds who live near tundra lakes in summer.*

skinny legs help them walk in the water to look for
food.

Lemmings are little plant-eaters that look like
mice. They live in tunnels on the arctic tundra.
Lemmings build nests of lichens, grass, and moss.

Arctic foxes and snowy owls hunt lemmings. The snowy owl's white feathers blend in with the white snow so lemmings do not see them coming. Arctic foxes have white coats in the winter and brown in the summer. Their furry coats blend in at any time of year.

△ A northern bog lemming

▲ *A snowy owl is barely seen against the snow.*

Snowshoe rabbits also change color with the seasons. In the winter, they are pure white, with ears tipped in black. As the weather warms, their white winter coats turn reddish-brown.

Snowshoe rabbits are actually hares. They are also called varying hares and arctic hares. When rabbits are born, they have no fur and their eyes are closed.

▽ A young snowshoe hare with its brown summer fur   △ An arctic fox in winter

Baby hares are born with fur coats and open eyes, however. Snowshoe babies have fur and their eyes are open too. They can hop when they are only three days old, and grow quickly.

Bighorn sheep, musk ox, and reindeer are the tundra's large animals. They all have thick fur. Bighorn sheep live in alpine areas. They move easily on high

▲ A male bighorn sheep, or ram

△ A herd of musk ox

mountain ledges. Musk ox travel the Arctic in herds. They chew on grass, lichens, and sedges as they travel. Large deer also live in the arctic tundra. They are called reindeer in Europe and Asia and caribou in North America. People there know the strength of the caribou. Caribou pull heavy sleds for long distances. Their wide hooves help them walk on snow and ice. People also value the animal's milk, meat, and hides.

▲ An Alaskan caribou

A Terrific Find

△ *A stuffed woolly mammoth in the Royal British Columbia Museum, Canada*

One of the biggest animals in the arctic tundra was the woolly mammoth. They looked like shaggy elephants with huge tusks. But woolly mammoths don't live on the tundra anymore. In 1997, a man named Zharkov was out walking in Russia's tundra. He saw something sticking up from the ground. It was the tusk of a mammoth.

Word spread of Zharkov's find. Scientists came out to see for themselves. They brought jackhammers to break up the permafrost around the animal. Then they

▲ *Loading the mammoth's huge tusks on a sled*

△ *A woolly mammoth's skull and tusks were found in the Black Hills of South Dakota.*

tunneled below it. They carved out a block of 20 tons of frozen mud with the mammoth inside.

By 1999, the scientists were ready to move the block. A helicopter lifted it out of the ground and took it to a laboratory. The scientists used hair dryers to thaw out the permafrost slowly. They named the mammoth Zharkov, after the man who discovered it.

▲ *Lifting Zharkov's woolly mammoth out by helicopter*

△ *People can see a woolly mammoth skeleton at the Yakutsk Museum in Russia.*

The scientists learned that when the male mammoth died, he was about forty years old. He had been frozen in ice for about 23,000 years.

Threats to the Tundra

The tundra is a tough place to live in. But in some ways it is very delicate. It is easy to throw natural life out of balance.

Some animals in the tundra eat only lemmings. If anything happens to the lemmings, these animals have nothing at all to eat. Some animals eat only plants. If anything damages the plants, these animals will go hungry. For example, caribou eat lichens all winter, when no other plants grow. They also munch on the reindeer moss that sprouts up through the snow. Today, however, reindeer moss picks up poisons in the air and rain from factories. Caribou become ill when they eat this lichen.

The tundra is a large place. Much of it is unexplored. Scientists know that many ancient animals must be buried in the permafrost. They know there must be other ancient lichens too. And they wonder

△ *The tundra is a harsh but delicate environment.*

what reindeer moss can tell us about air pollution. There is still much to be learned about this fascinating land called the tundra.

Glossary

bog—wet, spongy ground

evaporate—to rise into the air as a gas

permafrost—a layer of earth below the tundra's surface soil that is permanently frozen

pingos—low hills caused by permafrost

polygons—cracks in the land caused by the melting and freezing earth.

tree line—the area between the tundra and forest where plant and tree growth is short because of the cold, windy, dry weather

Did You Know?

- The word *tundra* is a Finnish or Russian word for "land of no trees."

- Tundra covers one-fifth of Earth's surface.

- In Canada, people call the tundra the Barrens.

- Because the winters are cold on the tundra, the animals breed and raise their young quickly during the short summers.

- On tundra land, people build houses and pipelines on stilts. That keeps heat from the structures from melting the permafrost and causing the ground to collapse.

At a Glance

Location: Far northern Asia, northern North America, northern Europe

Amount of rain or snow each year: 10 inches (25 centimeters)

Description: Flat, dry land with snow most of the year and permanently frozen land; only a few plants can survive

Common animals: Arctic foxes, caribou, lemmings, wolves, waterbirds

Common plants: Lichens, low shrubs, sedges, mosses, grasses

Want to Know More?

At the Library
Kaplan, Elizabeth. *The Tundra*. New York: Benchmark Books, 1996.
Steele, Philip. *Tundra*. Minneapolis: Carolrhoda Books, 1996.
Walsh Shepherd, Donna. *Tundra*. Danbury, Conn.: Franklin Watts,
    1996.

On the Web
The Polar World
http://www.ville.montreal.qc.ca/biodome/e2-coll/emp.htm
For a look at the tundra regions of the Arctic and the Antarctic

The Tundra Biome
http://lsb.syr.edu/projects/cyberzoo/biomes/tundra.html
For information about geological events, weather, and animals asso-
ciated with tundra

Through the Mail
Alaska Natural History Association
750 West Second Avenue, Suite 100
Anchorage, AK 99501-2167
For guidebooks, maps, and videos about alpine tundra

On the Road
Denali National Park and Preserve
P.O. Box 9
Denali Park, AK 99755
907/683-2294
To visit an alpine tundra for yourself

Index

About the Author

Susan H. Gray holds bachelor's and master's degrees in zoology from the University of Arkansas in Fayetteville. She has taught classes in general biology, human anatomy, and physiology. She has also worked as a freshwater biologist and scientific illustrator. In her twenty years as a writer, Susan H. Gray has covered many topics and written a variety of science books for children.